He Read to Us

Remembering Jess D. Wilson

poems by

E. Gail Chandler and T. Sammie Wakefield

Finishing Line Press
Georgetown, Kentucky

He Read to Us

For Ruth Wilson, our mother,
and Rebecca Jo Wilson, our sister

———————

Remembering Jess D. Wilson

*Jess Wilson was a writer, genealogist, historian,
community leader, mentor, Appalachian activist, and much
more. His career and accomplishments are well documented
elsewhere. These poems are about him as father, especially
when we were young and then again, in his last years—
times when our memories are most vivid.*

*Southeastern Kentucky has been named by some as a hard
place to live. We did not find it so because of our parents'
refusal to subscribe to stereotypes and negativity. They saw
the natural beauty of the land and story-telling heritage
of our people as opportunities to create magic. Being their
children has always been an adventure.*

ACKNOWLEDGMENTS

Thanks to the editors of the following publications in which these poems,
sometimes in different versions have appeared.

Heartland Review: "The Guardian," "Darmok and Jalard at Tanagra"
Pegasus: "He Read to Us," "Dinner at the Shanghai Blossom," "Offer," "Death at a
Mission School"
Golden Words: "Watching Birds"
Mississippi Poetry Journal: "Last Leaves," "Why There Is a Butt Print in the Phlox,"
"Farm for Sale," "The Choosing," "The Trail Home"
Where the Red Road Meets the Sky: "The Guardian," "Last Leaves" "Watching
Birds"
OPD Best of 2013: "Here It Is"
Poetry Virginia Review: "Death in a Mission School"

Thanks also to our friends and coaches at Green River Writers, Clear Creek
Writers, Western Kentucky University writing workshop, Hindman Settlement
School, and most especially Mary O'Dell.

Publisher: Leah Maines
Editor: Christen Kincaid
Cover Art: T. Sammie Wakefield
Author Photo of E. Gail Chandler: Mackenzie Dye
Author Photo of T. Sammie Wakefield: E. Gail Chandler
Cover Design: Elizabeth Maines

Printed in the USA on acid-free paper.
Order online: www.finishinglinepress.com
also available on amazon.com

Author inquiries and mail orders:
Finishing Line Press
P. O. Box 1626
Georgetown, Kentucky 40324
U. S. A.

Table of Contents

THE MAKING OF AN ENVIRONMENTALIST
1929

The week after Jess and Cousin Bill
dressed up and went to the city
for a 4-H conference
and found they were the only boys
in bib overalls

they went frog gigging.
The big moon brought luck
and they took their bag of frogs
back to Aunt Laurie's
for cleaning.

Jess cut off the legs
because he was the worker
and Bill was the talker
and Bill jawed long
about those overalls.

Jess rinsed the frog legs
under the yard pump
and threw the rest
over the fence
by the corn patch.

Next morning, the boys
found the back lawn covered
with crawling, croaking
cripples. They never
went gigging again.

Bill moved to Chicago,
became a VP of advertising
and played golf. Jess stayed
in the Appalachians, never shot a squirrel,
and moved terrapins off the tarmac.

THE END OF TIME IN CLAY COUNTY
In the 1930s

When the northern lights shone over Burning Springs,
all fluorescent green and yellow and red,
Henry Hignite switched on the sawmill siren
so everyone could see.

People poured out of their houses,
eyes bugging at the crazy sky.
They knew for sure, my daddy said,
that Gabriel had come.

HE READ TO US

The Swiss Family Robinson,
"The Most Dangerous Game,"
'The Tell-Tale Heart,"
"The Raven."

He never changed a diaper
or washed a plate
but bought Mom
the first dishwasher
in the county.

He stormed and thundered
when we didn't go to bed
on demand, once scrawled
7:00 PM on our bedroom wall
in letters two feet high.

But when he came home at night,
we raced to open his lunchbox.
We never knew what we'd find—
Little Debbies, a Hershey bar,
once even a baby rabbit.

EXTINCTION

Winding up that mountain
toward Pigeon Roost,
he'd tell us about migration,
how the ground would be pink
as far as you could see.

We'd reach the summit,
gaze upon the clapboard houses,
the Hilltop Drive-In and the junkyard
while dreaming fields of pigeons
on their way to Florida.

I thought he'd been there,
the way he'd walked
among the last American chestnuts,
even though he told us

about Martha, the last passenger pigeon,
who died in 1914 at the Cincinnati Zoo,
four years before he was born.

WORKING WITH MY FATHER
by T. Sammie Wakefield

> *The courage to do a project is more important
> than the knowledge of how to do it.*
>
> —*Jess Wilson*

With no brothers, I was his helper.
At ten I mastered switches and lights,
mixed mortar, nailed roof boards,
and stuffed insulation
into cobwebby spaces.

The night we moved into a four-room house
with a red-water well and a path,
he tore down a wall,
beginning the growth over twenty years
to ten rooms and a bath.

He tinkered for years with coal-fired heat.
Never content with usually-done;
sent me under the house with plastic and gravel
to cover the musty clay,
cut holes in the floor of each room
to let in a blast of warmth.

We built a three-part cistern
for filtering rain and pond water;
put a sink in all bedrooms,
and wired each appliance
to its own electric meter.

———————————————

My father leaned on his walker,
viewing my progress that sunlit day,
as I sewed, trimmed, and stapled
waterproof covers on his favorite chair.

*I see your fingers doing what I would do.
It's like watching my own hands.*

HIDDEN COMPARTMENTS

It is late that night they move,
the children cross, hungry,
boxes stacked half to the ceiling.

While she struggles with dinner,
finds toilet paper for the outhouse,
sheets for the beds,

he tears out a kitchen wall
and drywall dust drifts
over the chaos.

He builds his first hiding place
into the breakfast bar
of the remodeled kitchen

and the last, in a mountain cabin
behind the stairs, a spot to secure bourbon
from drunks and the young.

Later, when the children pack him up
for nursing care, stumble
upon a bedside cubby of secrets,

they long to find the niche,
the hole behind a shelf
where he left his memory.

SOMETIMES MY DADDY WORE A HARDHAT

Walking in the door, he'd take it off,
lay it on the kitchen counter
beside a lunchbox,
which we would treasure-search,

then I'd take up the hardhat,
push down the gliders
until the stained and sweaty head harness
fell free.

I'd drop the harness into a basin
of hot water and add Tide,
swish it around,
let it soak.

I'd sprinkle Ajax
on the hardhat,
scrub until it was white
inside and out.

I'd rinse it all in hot water,
dry the hat with a tea towel,
hang up the harness to dry,
then slide them back together.

Now the hardhat
is on a shelf.
It has no finish
because I'd scrubbed it off.

DEATH AT A MISSION SCHOOL

One May morning, they miss a boy.
By noon, the searchers' boat
rides low in the school farm pond.
My father arrives in a co-op truck
and they call to him. He remembers
baling wire in the depths, wire
his foot had touched thirty years prior,
the night before they expelled him
for taking a midnight swim.

They give Father a hooked pole
and in his hand, the probe touches firm,
catches cloth. He reaches into the water
and grabs hair. They hoist Johnny,
a coal miner's only son, onto the boat floor.

Johnny's twin sister did not return to school
and sometimes I take down the yearbook,
stare at the freckled nose, the dark hair,
the fourteen-year-old
below the words *In Memoriam.*

WHAT SHOULD A POET DO ABOUT HER ANCESTORS?

It took work and the Internet to find my mother's
Dutch lineage—the Frisian fishermen and the
Mennonite preacher, Romke Haitjema, who left for
the new world in 1853 to avoid the draft. And the
cousins I have in the Netherlands like the one who
named his daughter Saskia, after Rembrandt's wife.
On the other side, I grew up glutted with ancestors.
My father endlessly shared their stories. He also
gathered records on eastern Kentuckians back to
England and letters arrived from folks in forty-eight
states requesting information. It took six pickup loads
to move his records from a home office to a room
named for him at the Clay County Genealogical
Society. Now strangers sometimes email me with
ancestral puzzles. I send them to the society. I get
bogged down about the time Andy Baker played his
fiddle and I never have understood the feuds. I would
like to know more about a mixed-race foremother.
Then there is my high school best friend who was
adopted. We find out, years later, that she was a
Wilson from Owsley County. A cousin. Third
or fourth? I'll find out soon as I get back Daddy's
Phillip Wilson book I loaned out, the one he
annotated, reprinted.

HOW THEY LOST THEIR FATHER

The smell of marijuana floats
through the Ocho Rios marketplace
unnoticed by the couple celebrating
their sixtieth anniversary with three daughters.

Hey, mon, a lanky Jamaican
calls to the father, *this walking stick,*
I carve it myself. I sacrifice to you
for thirty American dollars.

The father shakes his head, walks away,
but thinks how fine the design,
how sore his feet.
After haggling, he buys it for ten.
The father spies a chair
owned by a round lady running a batik concession.
He buys a floppy red hat with yellow hibiscus flowers
and sinks into the offered seat.

Leaving him, the wife and daughters
browse teak bowls, sandalwood turtles
and have beads braided into their hair.
Arms full of parcels,
they return to the batik stand
but the old man is gone.

The round lady points.
The women walk fast in the soggy air
past coconut palms and carved pelicans,
through splotches of sunlight.
The wife says, *he just flops open his wallet,*
lets the bills hang out . . .
The daughters ask a leather vendor,
Have you seen our father?
He points. *The old mon, he went that way.*
They ask again and again.
Our father, our father
and the people smile and point.

They find him in a taxi
holding the carved walking stick
and wearing a floppy red hat.

MEMORIAL
by T. Sammie Wakefield

> *Some of these have left behind a name.....*
> *others have perished as though they had never been born.*
> *—Ecclesiasticus 44: 1-15*

Our father tore down a gated fence
dividing our Appalachian cemetery.
He did not like to segregate
neighbors of limited means
from those with headstones.

His granddaughter traveled
deeper south at twelve,
demanded to see the *other* graves,
saw rotting wooden crosses choked
in a weedy walled-off space.

On a New Hampshire glacial moraine,
my feet crunch blue-gray lichen
in the Carroll County poor-farm lot.
I study rows of numbered crumbling markers,
beginning at two, ending at two-hundred-ninety-eight.

No gate marks a dividing fence,
no portal for these northern paupers.
I am forced to straddle woven wire
strung between granite posts,
to reach manicured rows

where polished monuments
are covered with names.

THE GUARDIAN

On a path of brown pine needles,
my father trudges toward my sister and me,
holding a terrapin.

First one I've seen all year, he says.
*Before we built a road around this place
I counted thirty-seven one spring day.*

We nod wisely,
talk of weed killer,
acid rain, global warming.

He shakes his head. *It was the road,
the soft clay, made their eggs
easier for skunks to find.*

He turns the terrapin
as if it is a Ming vase,
shows us it's a female.

We watch his hands,
veins large, nails thick
knuckles big as plums.

LAST LEAVES

The woman holds her husband's arm
as they peer through bare December oaks
and down the mountain valley.
Don't grow old in the land where you were born,
he says, *there are too many ghosts.*

She doesn't say she was a girl herself
when she followed him here,
made these people hers
like Ruth in the Bible.

She recalls aloud their winter hikes
up steep hills, along ridges until at last,
they arrived at Grandma's or Aunt Bessie's,
warmed themselves by the coal grate,
ate pintos, onions and bread from new-ground corn.

And she ponders her address book,
how last spring she rewrote every line,
shook the dead people out.

HOW THE CONNUBIAL CRIB CAME TO POSSUM TROT

The new groom whined to the old couple
who had collected him, his wife and other strays,
wandering the hills, that something was missing.

He liked the deer, the wild turkeys,
the log cabin with a gritter on the wall,
also the six-sided camp building

where a Christian volunteer or a Vista worker, when tired
of poverty warring, might drink a beer or, after the old folks
went to bed, smoke something different on a Saturday night.

He admired the crusty old man who woke
his charges by ringing a cowbell,
declaring loud— twice— *The British are coming,*

until they tumbled from their beds,
faced the hangover, the eggs and bacon,
a day of pulling flat rocks from creeks,

building rock fences, roofing roofs,
or painting a rainbow green and purple.
But back to what wasn't perfect—

The young man said that not one bed
in the whole three hundred acres
was double.

So the next weekend,
the old man piled the troops into a truck,
drove (after a fashion, never using first gear)

to Great Aunt Hallie's, where they disassembled
an ancient corncrib, numbered the logs,
stacked them into the truck.

They furnished the cabin with shelves, books by Dickens
and John Fox, an Appalachian gourd woman's possum
with gray glued-on human hair,

and, of course, the required bed.

WATCHING BIRDS

He releases the lever on his Lazy Boy,
turns to the window and stares,
stroking the buttery leather with a gnarled hand.

His daughter, gray herself,
wonders if he needs a blanket
but asks what he thinks about the birds.

It musta been the spring before
I was three in August, he says,
maybe 1921. My first memory, I reckon.
The highway was just dirt ruts then,
never been a car in these parts.

I looked up and here comes
this crowd a people all walking
down the road.
Sunday, it was, and they'd been to church.
Grandma and Bessie and Mommy
cooked until three in the afternoon,
fed them every one.

His wife has heard this story
for over sixty years.
She picks up her mug of chamomile tea.
Your daughter asked you about birds.

He points to the half-empty feeder.
I was telling her.

CABO SAN LUCAS

We eat tomatoes,
tortillas, avocados,
drink tequila with salt and lime,
climb on a motorboat
singing "Margaritaville"
and ride toward the big rock,
wind fast in our faces,
water splashing
our tee shirts.

Our father stays behind
on the cruise ship, napping.
Yesterday this man
who'd always known the way
got lost walking to lunch.
His confused blue eyes
weigh on our day
but we aren't afraid.
Not yet.

WHY THERE'S A BUTT PRINT IN THE PHLOX

For their sixtieth anniversary,
she begged the children for a cruise,
not for romance
but an escape from certainty
and funerals.

They won Champagne
for the longest marriage.
Somewhere near Aruba, she asked him
to meet her for coffee.
He stumbled to the table an hour late,
pale, frightened,
unsure where he'd been.

Now they stay home with Pete,
the handyman,
and the telephone.

She gazes out the window
at creeping phlox swathing a creek-stone wall,
at her husband leaning on a cane, talking,
at Pete on his knees —
hands in black dirt planting purple star impatiens —
nodding as if he's listening.

The old man lifts his cane to make a point,
teeters, then flops onto the bench-high wall.
Lavender flowers drape his legs,
butterflies and bumblebees take flight.

My darling, she says,
turning from the window,
biting her lip.

DINNER AT THE SHANGHAI BLOSSOM

Yesterday, my sister and I arrived
at the cabin my father built
on land owned by his family since the Civil War,
land he first loved when he was two.

He was searching for a book,
the *Divine Comedy* illustrated by Gustave Doré,
the copy he bought in Harlan for a quarter,
the one with mouse teeth prints on the spine.

This morning, he thinks I am my sister,
asks six times what day it is.
Sometimes he forgets how to type,
can't remember how to use the remote.

At breakfast, we discuss du Maurier's *Rebecca*.
My middle-aged mind can't find the first line.
He says *Last night, I dreamed I went
to Manderley again.*

Later, at the independent living place,
we watch as Papa stares at the contract.
You'll have to shoot me, he says,
but he signs.

His wife of sixty-eight years
wants them to move here
and he won't deny her.

After paying the waiting list fees,
we eat at his favorite Chinese buffet.
Rice hangs in our throats.

FARM FOR SALE

I always thought they would crash
and kill each other at that farm,
Mom in her Honda, Dad in a dusty station wagon,
dashing toward retirement on blind curves.

But in their seventies, she still rode her bike
and at eighty they hiked the mountain
each morning, Thermos of coffee
and two mugs in his pack.

His cousin Billie recollected how, just married,
they'd go walking, holding hands,
sometimes sliding the sawdust pile,
looking happy while others worked.

I remember driving their gravel,
the crunch beneath the wheels,
no center line, a bend ahead,
dust settling on oaks and sassafras,

a canopy of trees tunneling into night.

THE CHOOSING

The dark angel breathing
down his collar, Pa tells the family
to clear his office, take what they want.
Next week he'll donate what's left.

They are not selfish enough,
the daughters, the granddaughters,
and the crates fill slowly.
The sons-in-law refuse to choose.
One fixes the old man's computer,
the other sorts his files.

The grown-up granddaughters
search for memories among photos,
giggle and point, can't be bothered
to look for first editions.

Middle daughter finally takes a worn copy
of Bill Mauldin's *Up Front*
and her younger sister is tentative
about the book of Doré etchings
and asks if someone else wants it more.

The eldest daughter glances at the clock,
looks around the still-full room.
She selects a leather-bound set
of Harvard Classics and celebrates
the fortune that gave her this family.

THE TRAIL HOME

Their cabin filled with boxes,
this last night of independent living,
my parents rock on the porch.
The creek burbles. The frogs sing.
We say *Sleep well.*
Tomorrow's a big day.

Beneath a mile of oak and poplar canopy,
my husband and I hike toward our camp.
A stag feeds at trail's edge.
Remembering a deer surprised,
a woman gored, I clap.

He leaps magnificent
against the blue-black sky
and bounds into the dusk.

On the other side of the farm
between our shelter
and the outhouse,
a wildcat pads up the hill
and pauses grey,
waiting for the humans to pass.

Next morning,
two wild turkeys
sprint across the path
and disappear into the pine.

CONSIDERING THE FAMILY CAMP
by T. Sammie Wakefield

> *It is a place for young people.*
> *They come for the magic.*
> *—My sister, Rebecca Jo*

The mown green trails lead them on.
They do not know
the warp speed of blackberry stalks
and sourwood sprouts
woven with wefts of saw-briars and vines.

They do not know
the desire of wood
to mulch on the forest floor,
how quickly bugs and mold entice
frames to sag and droop.

Their sleek strong bodies
leap high and land on springy knees.
They do not know
that muscles stiffen, bones leach,
joints and tendons grind.

Names roll off young tongues,
gliding out smoothly.
They do not know
once-supple brains can tangle
and memories of great loves grow dim.

They do not know
the body's deep hunger for earth,
that it wills away each action
until blinking and breathing
are gone.

OFFER

My ears are full of spring—
peepers, sparrows, wind in the pines.

How can we sell this land, break ties
with these sad and wicked hills,
our Scots-Irish and Cherokee blood
mingled with this red water
and its smell of devil's sulfur?

How can we sell the four deer
who stood on the gray gravel lane
just past dawn,
the wild turkeys and their parade
of flapping young, the wildcat screaming
like a mortal in the pangs of birth?

Will this couple relax in the porch swing
and admire the fieldstone chimney?
See the shadow that the poplar
casts across the lake?

Yet this must be right.
Sister needs a roof,
Father, nursing care,
and we, a first floor bedroom
for when we can no longer climb the stairs.

PRICED TO SELL
Log cabin, land owned by one family since the Civil War

Sister tapes a ceiling crack,
plasters, sands and paints.
My husband stacks paint pans,
sweeps the porch.

Sister and I climb on chairs,
remove heavy pottery from oak shelves,
scrub the planks, wash the dishes,
replace them, eye the result.

We burn spice candles,
take down picture—
a child with a terrapin,
a grey woman churning.

Two days later, we gather
with the buyers and agents
around a table in the sunroom.
Papers move from hand to hand.

Pete, the handyman who worked
for my father twenty-four years,
appears in the doorway, smelling of drink.
He stares, turns, slips away.

On the mountainside,
two deer prance up a trail.
Pete's beagle emerges behind them,
barking, and they also disappear.

NO DIVING OR JUMPING

Two old men stand on the pier,
pointing at the sign, laughing.
These cousins once sat in Granny's kitchen
side by side in handmade highchairs.

Today one uses a walker,
the other will within the year.
They were boarding school roommates,
mountain men, first in their families to attend college.

Their eyes are blue as the sea and they
profile the sky with long, straight noses.
Each stood best man at the other's wedding.
Their firstborns came a month apart.

One was driven a thousand miles
for this visit, and they both know
they will never see the ocean again.

HERE IT IS

My dad gives me his copy
of *Tales from the Arabian Nights.*
He reaches for a pen and writes,
To my daughter, then stops.
He looks up, his large blue eyes
searching my face for clues.
The dehumidifier roars.
A statue of a long-necked Maasai
stares out from a shelf. The blue spruce
outside the window is dropping its needles.
A brass lamp gleams as he squints
and adds, From her loving father,
studying each word.

MY FATHER'S HAT

The stingy-brimmed one
I got him in Zambia,
made in China
and covered with
lion paw tracks.

He wore it every day
—for a while—
to protect his freckled
Scots-Irish face
from East Kentucky sun.

It replaced the fedora
adorned with hibiscus flowers
he bought from the vendor-woman
in Jamaica who offered him a chair
when his feet gave out,

back when he was eighty or so
and using a computer,
about the time he started
an Internet mailing list
called *A Thousand and One Nights,*

back when he could do so many things.

RHIZOME

Sometime after he got lost
on a cruise ship
but before clinging
to his stories with my teeth,
I cancel his accident policy,
knowing death by truck
or falling off a roof is unlikely.
I call the funeral director Pa wants—
the one he used to joke always
inquired about his health—
to know what to expect.
My gaze wanders to the old aloe plant
whose babies can die
when separated from the parent.

NOT FOR BETTER
For Mama

If upon waking, you find him still
and with the light escaped,
can you hold him and remember
the rainbow and the dusty road?

Can you forget his fading body?
The urine and feces on the rug?
The questions like a mantra—
What day is it? What time is lunch?

Today his blue eyes fill with terror
and he says he is insane.
You know he feels the valleys
where his mind used to be.

Rain pounds against the window.
The drops soak into the ground.
Some nights his breathing falters,
stops but then returns.

ADVICE IN THE SEASON OF HOSPICE
by T. Sammie Wakefield

Make room in all travel
for the funeral clothes.
Avoid staying one step away
from the experience.
The moving walkway is nearing its end—
attend to children
and mind your step.

I enter the place called nursing care.
Does he know me?
Does he know I am his middle child—
the one called Baby Doll
when I was small?

This is a time of withdrawal.
He will sleep a lot.
Not eating or drinking is a sign
          of the body shutting down.
You may read to him
          from the stories he wrote.

I read the tales we have heard and heard
 in the mountain rhythm he knows.
At the punch lines he laughs—
          a rare and good sound.

Back at the house we sort clothes, pictures, dishes,
cards from holidays past.
A cousin lugs three black bags to Goodwill
before we can sort again,
before we can change our minds.

I take his best suit to the cleaners,
find a shirt and tie.
We do these tasks now afraid that later
          we'll be too consumed with sorrow,
as if this prolonged season
is not already grief.

The moving walkway is nearing its end—
attend to children
and mind your step.

FEBRUARY MORNING

Brushing aside the curtain
closed against the draft,

she finds iced trees, new snow,
limbs across the drive.

If her father dies this day,
they'll shiver on that mountain,

the preacher's careful words
only noise

while they plan escape
to warm cars and casseroles.

But then how sad to go in April.

THE LAST TIME MY FATHER LAUGHED
by T. Sammie Wakefield

The hospice nurse said
A month at most.
His face was thin
with jaw-line moved north
from loss of teeth.
A hearing aid and glasses arm
perched on the remnant of his good ear,
assisting as they could
these weak portals
to the outside world.
He sat dozing in his Geri-chair,
holding my mother's hand.

I told a story:
Remember, Daddy, when we lived at Gray Hawk?
We were putting up corn out in the yard.
I was ten, my hands too weak to break off shucks from the cob.
I used a butcher knife as cleaver,
chipped off a hunk from the side of my finger.
I reached down to retrieve that bit of me—
just as a hen gobbled it up.
I didn't wash dishes for two weeks,
and we ate that chicken.

His face crinkled.
He laughed loud, long,
then sighed,
closed his eyes
and sank into that place
we cannot follow.

AFTER

I am in one of those airport seats
where strangers wait, search faces
and watch people they don't love
hug and drag suitcases.
My cell phone rings.

He just stopped breathing.
The nurse checked his heart.
They are giving us time.
Mama is holding his head.
He's still warm.
Little sister's voice is thick.

My fingers mash wrong buttons
searching for the funeral home.
I call a cousin, check Google,
find the number, tell the director
to send someone.
Do you want to see him first?
I don't.

Then my other sister walks
through security. She searches my face.
and knows. We embrace, then details
fall out like evening news.

She doesn't want to see him either.
She'd been at his bed ten days ago,
a moment when his dementia lifted.
She'd made him laugh.
That's the memory she wants.

We have avocado salad
at an airport bistro
and each drink a glass of wine.

THE END

We didn't buy a coffin
with comfort coils
though I was briefly tempted
by some stained oak wood.

Cheap, I told a funeral home man.
It's what Daddy wanted.
I know he'd not be happy
about the embalming and the viewing

but it's what everyone expects.
Then he told us not to announce the meal,
just have the preacher
say it at the end. *If you put it in the paper,*

poor folks will pour out of the hills
and eat up all the food.
We're in eastern Kentucky, after all.
I handed him the obit, said I put cremation in it.

He frowned. And the *Herald Leader*
named the cemetery
but said *burial arrangements*
instead of scattered.

The funeral home people left the casket
open during the service, not Daddy's wish.
I stopped on the way out, told him
I was sorry, that I had tried my best.

But Mama said it was okay,
that he got to hear Cousin Sam
say those nice things and got to be
the center of what was going on.

A few days later, the postman
brought a box. I opened it,
rubbed the rough ashes through my fingers
and understood why he joined

the Funeral Consumers Alliance.
We'll all be like this in a hundred years
and he never was a patient man.

DARMOK AND JALAD AT TANAGRA

*The Tamarians spoke entirely by metaphor, referencing
mythological and historical people and events from their culture.*
—Star Trek, The Next Generation

One of the sympathy cards said
Sorry to hear about your dad.
I know you were so close.

Close? Strange word, for I don't recall
a real talk in seventy years.
He spoke in story.

Close? When I look at my feet,
I see his feet. My hands are his hands.
His smell is on my pillow.

When I told Mama a joke
I waited to hear
Your dad already told me.

And when my family says
You're just like him, I know
I'm in charge or trying

to be in charge or ignoring
others' wishes or demanding
or guiding them to my own particular
                    conclusion.

But when he died they liked
that I called the funeral home,
wrote the obituary,

made the slide show,
and stored his ashes
in my garage until spring.

ECHOES

A door blows open.
It's Daddy, sister says.

I awake to him singing
Goodnight Irene, Goodnight Irene
I'll see you in my dreams.

The phone rings.
Hello, a man says. And my name.
A voice distinct as that patch of hills,
familiar as my face.
But it's just Roger, my cousin.

Mama talks to Daddy every day.
She says that since we took his ashes
to the family graveyard, he's happier.
Now he helps her wash the dishes
and fold the clothes.

E. Gail Chandler's poems and short stories have appeared in numerous regional publications plus the journals *Passager* and *Verse Wisconsin*; the anthologies *Motif, Standing on the Mountain: Voices of Appalachia,* and *Bigger than they Appear.* She received a Betty Gabehart prize for poetry, *Appalachian Heritage's* Denny Plattner award, and was nominated by Verse Wisconsin for The Best of the Web. She has a nonfiction book, *Sunflowers on Market Street*, and a poetry chapbook, *Where the Red Road Meets the Sky.* Chandler has degrees from Berea College in Kentucky and from The New School in New York City. She served three years in the Marine Corps during the Vietnam era. In 1976, she became the first female deputy warden in a male prison in Kentucky and worked in corrections until retirement. She lives by a lake in Shelbyville, Kentucky with her husband, Curtis Chandler, a psychologist. They have a daughter, Tara.

T. Sammie Wakefield has a degree in Art from Berea College and in Occupational Therapy from Texas Woman's University. She creates wood sculptures, repairs and re-homes vintage sewing machines, and as a retired occupational therapist, continues her specialty in seating and mobility, doing volunteer wheelchair clinics in Peru with an NGO called Eleanore's Project. She has been writing poetry for four years, and this is her first publication. She lives in Moultonborough, New Hampshire in an 1820 Cape Cod House with her husband, Richard Wakefield. They have a daughter, Esther.

CPSIA information can be obtained
at www.ICGtesting.com
Printed in the USA
LVOW12s0610231116
514215LV00002B/43/P